Delve into this box of stories a[...] grows as big as a hippopotamus[...] wooden chest overflowing with[...] love to dance, a giant who thinks boys would make a very tasty dinner, and many other strange and exciting people and animals.

No story has been put in the box without very careful inspection by children's book specialist Pat Thomson. All the stories are tried and tested favourites, and all by top authors – including Joan Aiken, Beverly Cleary, Jamila Gavin and Alison Uttley.

You won't want to stop reading until you get right to the bottom of the box!

PAT THOMSON is a well-known author and anthologist. Additionally she works as a lecturer and librarian in a teacher training college – work which involves a constant search for short stories which have both quality and child-appeal. She is also an Honorary Vice-President of the Federation of Children's Book Groups. She is married with two grown-up children and lives in Northamptonshire.

A BOX

of Stories for Six Year Olds

Collected by Pat Thomson

Illustrated by Phillip Norman

CORGI BOOKS

A BOX FULL OF STORIES FOR SIX YEAR OLDS
A CORGI BOOK : 0 552 54537 6

First published in Great Britain by Doubleday,
a division of Transworld Publishers Ltd.

PRINTING HISTORY
Doubleday edition published 1997
Corgi edition published 1998

Corgi Books are published by Transworld Publishers Ltd,
61–63 Uxbridge Road, Ealing, London W5 5SA,
in Australia by Transworld Publishers (Australia) Pty Ltd,
15–25 Helles Avenue, Moorebank, NSW 2170
and in New Zealand by Transworld Publishers (NZ) Ltd,
3 William Pickering Drive, Albany, Auckland.

Printed and bound in Great Britain by
Cox & Wyman Ltd, Reading, Berkshire.

Acknowledgements

The editor and publisher are grateful for permission to include the following copyright material in this anthology:

Joan Aiken, 'The Baker's Cat'. From *A Necklace of Raindrops*. First published by Jonathan Cape, 1968. Copyright Joan Aiken © 1968. Reprinted by permission of A.M. Heath & Company Ltd.

Beverly Cleary, 'The Quarrel'. From *Ramona and Her Mother*. First published by Hamish Hamilton Children's Books, 1979. Copyright Beverly Cleary © 1979. Reprinted by permission of Penguin Books Ltd.

Stan Cullimore, 'How to Become a Nicer Person'. From *Henrietta and the Tooth Fairy*. First published by Piccadilly Press Ltd, 1991. Copyright Stan Cullimore © 1991. Reprinted by permission of Piccadilly Press Ltd.

Dorothy Edwards, 'The Giant Who Wanted to Eat Boys'. From *The Magician Who Kept a Pub*. First published by Kestrel Books, 1975. Copyright Dorothy Edwards © 1975. Reprinted by permission of Penguin Books Ltd.

Nicholas Fisk, 'The Froggy Princess'. From *Pob's Stories,* ed. Anne Wood. First published by Fontana Young Lions, 1986. Copyright Nicholas Fisk © 1986. Reprinted by permission of the Laura Cecil Literary Agency.

Jamila Gavin, 'Kamla's Secret'. From *Kamla and Kate*. First published by Methuen Children's Books, 1983. Copyright Jamila Gavin © 1983. Reprinted by permission of David Higham Associates Ltd.

Moira Miller, 'Gran's New House'. From *What Size is Andy?* First published by Methuen Children's Books, 1984. Copyright Moira Miller © 1984. Reprinted by permission of Reed Consumer Books Ltd.

CONTENTS

The Baker's Cat   **1**
by Joan Aiken

How to Become a Nicer Person   **13**
by Stan Cullimore

Gran's New House   **23**
by Moira Miller

An Honest Penny   **33**
a retelling of a Scandinavian tale
by Pat Thomson

Kamla's Secret   **45**
by Jamila Gavin

The Froggy Princess   61
by Nicholas Fisk

The Quarrel   67
by Beverly Cleary

The Giant Who Wanted to Eat Boys   89
by Dorothy Edwards

The Hurricane Tree   105
by Libby Purves

Orion Hardy   115
by Alison Uttley

The Baker's Cat

Once there was an old lady, Mrs Jones, who
lived with her cat, Mog. Mrs Jones kept a
baker's shop, in a little tiny town, at the bottom
of a valley between two mountains.

Every morning you could see Mrs Jones's
light twinkle out, long before all the other
houses in the town, because she got up very
early to bake loaves and buns and jam tarts and
Welsh cakes.

First thing in the morning Mrs Jones lit a
big fire. Then she made dough, out of water
and sugar and yeast. Then she put the dough

into pans and set it in front of the fire to rise.

Mog got up early too. *He* got up to catch mice. When he had chased all the mice out of the bakery, he wanted to sit in front of the warm fire. But Mrs Jones wouldn't let him, because of the loaves and buns there, rising in their pans.

She said, 'Don't sit on the buns, Mog.'

The buns were rising nicely. They were getting fine and big. That is what yeast does. It makes bread and buns and cakes swell up and get bigger and bigger.

As Mog was not allowed to sit by the fire, he went to play in the sink.

Most cats hate water, but Mog didn't. He loved it. He liked to sit by the tap, hitting the drops with his paw as they fell, and getting water all over his whiskers!

What did Mog look like? His back, and his sides, and his legs down as far as where his socks would have come to, and his face and ears and his tail were all marmalade coloured. His stomach and his waistcoat and his paws were white. And he had a white tassel at the tip of his tail, white fringes to his ears, and white whiskers. The water made his marmalade fur go almost fox colour and his paws and waistcoat shining-white clean.

But Mrs Jones said, 'Mog, you are getting too excited. You are shaking water all over my pans of buns, just when they are getting nice and big. Run along and play outside.'

Mog was affronted. He put his ears and tail down (when cats are pleased they put their ears and tails *up*) and he went out. It was raining hard.

A rushing, rocky river ran through the middle of the town. Mog went and sat *in* the water and looked for fish. But there were no fish in that part of the river. Mog got wetter and wetter. But he didn't care. Presently he began to sneeze.

Then Mrs Jones opened her door and called, 'Mog! I have put the buns in the oven. You can come in now, and sit by the fire.'

Mog was so wet that he was shiny all over, as if he had been polished. As he sat by the fire he sneezed nine times.

Mrs Jones said, 'Oh dear, Mog, are you catching cold?'

She dried him with a towel and gave him some warm milk with yeast in it. Yeast is good for people when they are poorly.

Then she left him sitting in front of the fire and began making jam tarts. When she had put the tarts in the oven she went out shopping, taking her umbrella.

But what do you think was happening to Mog?

The yeast was making him rise.

As he sat dozing in front of the lovely warm fire he was growing bigger and bigger.

First he grew as big as a sheep.

Then he grew as big as a donkey.

Then he grew as big as a cart-horse.

Then he grew as big as a hippopotamus.

By now he was too big for Mrs Jones's little kitchen, but he was *far* too big to get through the door. He just burst the walls.

When Mrs Jones came home with her shopping-bag and her umbrella she cried out, 'Mercy me, what is happening to my house?'

4

The whole house was bulging. It was swaying. Huge whiskers were poking out of the kitchen window. A marmalade-coloured tail came out of the door. A white paw came out of one bedroom window, and an ear with a white fringe out of the other.

5

'Morow?' said Mog. He was waking up from his nap and trying to stretch.

Then the whole house fell down.

'Oh, Mog!' cried Mrs Jones. '*Look* what you've done.'

The people in the town were very astonished when they saw what had happened. They gave Mrs Jones the Town Hall to live in, because they were so fond of her (and her buns). But they were not so sure about Mog.

The Mayor said, 'Suppose he goes on growing and breaks our Town Hall? Suppose he turns fierce? It would not be safe to have him in the town, he is too big.'

Mrs Jones said, 'Mog is a gentle cat. He would not hurt anybody.'

'We will wait and see about that,' said the Mayor. 'Suppose he sat down on someone? Suppose he was hungry? What will he eat? He had better live outside the town, up on the mountain.'

So everybody shouted, 'Shoo! Scram! Pssst! Shoo!' and poor Mog was driven outside the town gates. It was still raining hard. Water was rushing down the mountains. Not that Mog cared.

But poor Mrs Jones was very sad. She began making a new lot of loaves and buns in the Town Hall, crying into them so much that the dough was too wet, and very salty.

Mog walked up the valley between the two mountains. By now he was bigger than an elephant – almost as big as a whale! When the sheep on the mountain saw him coming, they were scared to death and galloped away. But he took no notice of them. He was looking for fish in the river. He caught lots of fish! He was having a fine time.

By now it had been raining for so long that Mog heard a loud, watery roar at the top of the valley. He saw a huge wall of water coming towards him. The river was beginning to flood, as more and more rainwater poured down into it, off the mountains.

Mog thought, 'If I don't stop that water, all these fine fish will be washed away.'

So he sat down, plump in the middle of the

valley, and he spread himself out like a big, fat cottage loaf.

The water could not get by.

The people in the town had heard the roar of the flood-water. They were very frightened. The Mayor shouted, 'Run up the mountains before the water gets to the town, or we shall all be drowned!'

So they all rushed up the mountains, some on one side of the town, some on the other.

What did they see then?

Why, Mog, sitting in the middle of the valley. Beyond him was a great lake.

'Mrs Jones,' said the Mayor, 'can you make your cat stay there till we have built a dam across the valley, to keep all that water back?'

'I will try,' said Mrs Jones. 'He mostly sits still if he is tickled under his chin.'

So for three days everybody in the town took turns tickling Mog under his chin with hay-rakes. He purred and purred and purred. His purring made big waves roll right across the lake of flood-water.

All this time the best builders were making a great dam across the valley.

People brought Mog all sorts of nice things to eat, too — bowls of cream and condensed milk, liver and bacon, sardines, even chocolate! But he was not very hungry. He had eaten so much fish.

On the third day they finished the dam. The town was safe.

The Mayor said, 'I see now that Mog is a gentle cat. He can live in the Town Hall with you, Mrs Jones. Here is a badge for him to wear.'

The badge was on a silver chain to go round his neck. It said MOG SAVED OUR TOWN.

So Mrs Jones and Mog lived happily ever after in the Town Hall. If you should go to the little town of Carnmog you may see the policeman holding up the traffic while Mog walks through the streets on his way to catch fish in the lake for breakfast. His tail waves above the houses and his whiskers rattle against the upstairs windows. But people know he will not hurt them, because he is a gentle cat.

He loves to play in the lake and sometimes he gets so wet that he sneezes. But Mrs Jones is not going to give him any more yeast.

He is quite big enough already!

This story is by Joan Aiken.

How to Become a Nicer Person

'What on earth do you think you're doing, Henrietta?' shouted Dad.

Henrietta stopped and smiled at her father.

'I'm skipping. Watch.' She began to skip once more. Her father's face went bright red, like it always did when he got cross.

'I know you're skipping, Henrietta,' he sighed. 'But why are you using two of Daniel's ties as a skipping rope?'

'Because one tie isn't long enough on its own. So I had to put two together.' Henrietta carried on jumping.

Her father gasped. Henrietta noticed his teeth were now clenched and he spoke very slowly.

'What! You know better than to use Daniel's ties as a skipping rope. And I've told you before not to take anything from Daniel's room without asking first. Get to your room this instant. And don't come out until you've learnt how to behave properly.' He grabbed the ties. Henrietta stomped upstairs.

When she got to her room Henrietta slammed the door and yanked open the cupboard.

'This is going to be really boring,' she groaned. 'Now what do I do?' She began to rummage through her toys. 'Hello. What's this?' A book had fallen down the back of the shelf and been forgotten. Henrietta picked it up. It was called *How to Become a Nicer Person*. Henrietta opened it and in spite of herself, began to read. According to the man who wrote it, the easiest way to become a nicer person was to do three good deeds every day.

'I could do that,' thought Henrietta. 'Easy.'
She looked at herself in the mirror and smiled
her nicest smile.

'If I was to become a nicer person then I
would know how to behave properly.'

She decided that Dad would have cooled
down by now. So she put down the book and
went into the kitchen to begin her three good
deeds.

★

'Good afternoon, Daniel dearest,' she said to her sensible brother, who was carefully feeding Baby-Rose banana and baked beans. Daniel did not reply. He was far too busy. He didn't even look up when Henrietta spoke. Henrietta was just about to stick out her tongue and pull a horrible face to make Baby-Rose cry, when she remembered her book and the three good deeds. She smiled.

'Do let me help you, Daniel.' Before Daniel knew what was happening Henrietta had snatched the spoon and was feeding Baby-Rose all by herself.

'Thank you, Henrietta,' said Daniel, surprised and pleased. 'My *Computer World* has just arrived and there's something new I've got to figure out.'

Henrietta waved her hand. 'Off you go then. You enjoy yourself while I stay here and do all the work.'

'You sound just like Mum,' muttered Daniel as he opened his *Computer World* and began to read.

★

The trouble was that Henrietta was not as careful as her brother.

'Ratburgers,' she muttered as the baked beans slithered from the spoon on to the floor.

'Watch it,' yelled Daniel as a bit of banana plopped neatly on to the centre of his *Computer World*.

Baby-Rose laughed. Henrietta lifted her out of the high-chair and left the disaster area.

'For my next good deed,' thought Henrietta, 'I shall make Mum a nice hot cup of tea in her favourite mug. She loves tea.' The trouble was that Henrietta could not find any teabags. She found the Bovril jar though. So she used Bovril instead.

Her mother was in the garden mowing the lawn.

'Thank you, Henrietta. A nice hot cup of tea. My favourite.' Henrietta beamed.

'I know it is, Mum. I made it just the way you like.' She skipped back into the house. Her mother took a sip of the tea and squawked.

'Yuk. This tea tastes of Bovril. I hate Bovril.'

★

In the kitchen Henrietta was dancing around the table.

'Yippee,' she cried, 'now I have done two good deeds. Only one more and then I will be a nicer person. And even Dad won't be cross with me any more.' She wondered what to do next. Suddenly she had an idea.

'I'll tidy my room,' she cried. 'Dad always says it's so messy it's like a pigsty.' Henrietta went into her room and closed the door.

Soon everything was neat and tidy. There weren't any banana skins under the pillow. Henrietta had put them all in the binbag. She had even swept her collection of crisp packets from under the bed. And her dirty clothes were in the laundry basket.

'There,' said Henrietta as some dust floated past her nose. 'Finished. Now I have done three good deeds. I've fed Baby-Rose her dinner. I've made Mum a cup of tea and I've tidied my room. That means I've become a nicer ah . . . nicer ah . . . Oh no. Not my sneezy nose.' She tried to stop it. But it was too late.

'Atishoo.' She did a Henrietta hyper-sneeze that blew the binbag right out of the window. 'Oh good! Now I won't have to carry all that rubbish out to the dustbin.'

The door opened.

'Hello,' said Dad. He looked around the room and his face brightened. 'I must have walked into the wrong room, this can't possibly be yours, Henrietta. It's too tidy.'

'Dad,' cried Henrietta. 'I've done it.'

'Done what?' asked Dad.

'My three good deeds. I found a book that said if you want to become a nicer person you have to do three good deeds every day. And I have. So I've become a nicer person. So now I'll know how to behave properly, won't I?'

*

Just then Daniel appeared.

'I can't read my *Computer World*,' he wailed. 'The pages are stuck together with banana.'

Then Henrietta and her father went into the kitchen, where Henrietta's mother was pouring the contents of her cup down the sink.

'Worst cup of tea I've ever had.' She pulled a face. 'And you should see what's in the garden. It looks as if someone has emptied a binbag full of crisp packets all over my lovely lawn.' Everyone rushed to the window.

'Oh,' said Henrietta, 'that's where all my rubbish went.'

'By the way, what were your three good deeds, Henrietta?' asked Dad. Henrietta looked at the messy lawn. She looked at Daniel's *Computer World* stuck together with banana and she looked at the mug still in her mother's hand.

'My three good deeds,' she said. 'Hmm, well . . . they weren't really that good. In fact, I've decided not to do any more good deeds. I don't want to become a nicer person. It's too much like hard work. And it never comes out the way you want it to.'

Dad laughed, 'But what about your book?'

Henrietta shrugged her shoulders. 'I'll give it to Daniel, he needs it more than I do.'

With that she kissed her father. Then she

rushed up the stairs. She had just thought of a brilliant game to play with Daniel's ties! But this time she would ask him first.

This story is by Stan Cullimore.

Gran's New House

For as long as everyone could remember Gran had always lived in the same upstairs-downstairs, joined-onto-next-door house at the end of the road where the bus turned. The garden was full of huge clumps of flowers and bushes where the children played hide-and-seek or soldiers.

'I like your garden, Gran,' said Andy. 'It's all jungly!'

'Humph,' said Gran. 'It's far too big. I can't look after it like I used to.'

Tivvy, Dave and Dad went along at the weekends sometimes and helped her to tidy up and cut the grass. The lawnmower was too heavy for Andy, but he could help Gran in the house.

'Burummmmmmmm!' he roared, shoving the vacuum cleaner under the bed. 'Here comes the Gobble-Monster!'

'You're a real Handy Andy,' said Gran. 'You're just like your grandad used to be.'

Andy didn't remember his grandad. He looked at the photograph of the fat man with the bald head and white moustache that sat on Gran's sideboard and giggled.

'I don't look like that, Gran,' he said.

'Oh yes you do, sunshine,' said Gran, hugging him.

One day when they went to see Gran she had a letter to show them.

'I'm moving to a new house,' she said. 'One of those little ones near the shopping centre that are specially built for old people.'

'They're lovely, Gran,' said Mum. 'But very small. I don't know where you'll put all your furniture.'

'About time I got rid of some of it,' said

Gran. 'Too much polishing.'

'They don't have any stairs to slide down,' said Andy.

'Good thing too!' said Gran.

'Won't you miss the garden?' said Tivvy.

'No more weeds,' said Gran. She was really pleased about the new house.

When it was ready for her to move in, Dad borrowed a van to shift her furniture and everyone helped to pack.

Tivvy and Mum were upstairs folding up

sheets and blankets. Dad and Dave crawled about the living room taking the tacks out of the carpet.

Crash! Gran dropped a saucer in the kitchen.

'What happened?' called Mum from the top of the stairs.

'I've changed my mind,' said Gran. 'I don't want to go.'

'Oh come on,' said Dad, crawling out into the hall. 'You'll not have the garden to worry about, remember?'

'I'll miss my flowers,' said Gran, slowly packing her best vase in newspaper.

'You won't have all these stairs to run up and down,' said Mum, puffing into the kitchen with a box full of sheets.

'I'll miss my old bedroom,' said Gran.

'But there's new people moving in here, Gran!' said Andy. Tivvy poked him in the back.

'Stop it!' she hissed.

'They won't polish my letter-box,' grumbled Gran. 'Not properly.'

'Course they will,' said Mum. 'Let's have a quick cup of tea and then we'll finish packing the dishes.'

Everyone helped to carry the furniture out to the van. Dave and Tivvy lifted a little chest of drawers down from the bedroom. Andy tried to help Dad move the dressing table, but it was far too heavy for him.

'Tell you what, Andy,' said Gran. 'You'd better carry my plant. Todger's too small. He might drop it.' Andy held out his arms and Gran lifted down the big green plant that stood in the china pot in the front window. Andy had never seen the window without it.

'Be careful with that now,' said Gran. 'It's a lot older than you are.'

Andy walked very slowly down the path to the van, carrying Gran's plant. It was like being in a jungle; he could just see where he was going through the leaves. Todger followed him with two cushions from the settee, and Mum and Dad carried a rolled-up carpet.

At last when everything was loaded Gran put on her coat and hat and looked round the

27

empty living room. Andy stood beside her. He slipped his hand into hers.

'You can see where all the pictures were,' he said. The sun had faded the wallpaper, leaving brightly coloured patches. There was a big one for the flower painting over the settee and smaller ones where all the photographs had been. Andy could see the little square that had been his school photograph beside Gran's chair.

'They're all gh-o-o-o-osts!' said Dave in a spooky voice.

'Oh dear . . .' said Gran.

'Don't be silly, Dave,' said Mum, bouncing into the room. 'Come on, let's get moving.' She helped Gran, Andy and Todger into the van with Dad. She was walking round to the new house with Dave and Tivvy, pushing Rosie in the pram.

'Come on,' said Dad, bundling Gran into the van. 'Hurry up, Andy!'

Andy pushed the letter-box open with the tip of his finger.

'Goodbye, house,' he whispered into the

28

empty hall, and turned and ran back down the path to the van.

It took the rest of the day to move Gran's furniture into the new house. There seemed to be twice as many boxes and chairs as there had been before.

'It's too small,' said Gran. 'I knew it was a mistake. I don't like it!'

'It'll be all right, Gran. You'll see,' said Dad. He was back down on his knees again, banging nails into the hall carpet.

In the kitchen Mum was putting dishes into cupboards and Rosie was crawling round, banging pots and pans together. Tivvy and Dave were thumping around in the bedroom. Todger had found a big empty cupboard in the hall.

'Boo!' he shouted, jumping out and banging the door shut. Andy ignored him; he was poking at a hole in the bottom of Gran's old armchair.

Gran walked into the kitchen. She still had her coat and hat on.

'I'm not staying, you know,' she said.

'I don't like it.'

'Come on, Gran,' said Mum. 'It'll be better once we're sorted out.' She lifted Rosie from among the muddle of pots and pans on the floor and put her outside in the pram.

'Dave! Tivvy!' she called. 'You two pop down to the shops and bring back a cake for tea – and a bunch of flowers for Gran's vase.'

Dad put down his hammer and pulled Todger out of the hall cupboard.

'Pack that in!' he said. 'Or I'll nail you down under the carpet.'

'There, that's better already,' said Mum. 'At least it's quieter.'

'Well . . .' said Gran.

'Look! Look what I've found,' shouted Andy jumping up. 'There's some things in the bottom of the chair.'

He wiggled in his finger and out came a pencil, a few coins, a knitting needle and an old photograph in a small frame.

'Well, bless me!' said Gran. 'What have you got there? Let's have a look.'

Andy handed her the photograph. He had

never seen it before. It was a picture of a little
boy on a beach. He was wearing a dark suit
with a white collar like a sailor. His feet were
bare and his long trousers were rolled right up.
He was digging a sandcastle and had stopped
to smile at the camera.

'Good gracious!' said Mum, laughing at the
picture. The little boy with the curly hair and
the funny freckled nose laughed back.

'Fancy finding that again,' said Gran. 'I lost it

years ago! That's your grandad, that is.' Dad looked at the picture and laughed.

'It looks exactly like Andy,' he said. And so it did — even Andy could see that. Dad hammered two tacks into the wall beside the fireplace, just where Gran's chair would go.

He hung Grandad's photograph on one and Andy's on the other. The two little boys looked as if they were smiling at each other. Dad put Gran's chair beside them and she sat down and looked at the pictures for a long time.

'I am glad you found it,' she said at last. 'I always liked that little picture so much. You are clever, Andy!' She hugged him very tightly.

'Wasn't me,' said Andy, squeezed against her coat. 'It was moving to a new house.'

'That's true!' said Gran. She looked round at the table set ready for tea, her best vase waiting for a bright bunch of flowers and the two photographs smiling side by side, and she unbuttoned her coat.

This story is by Moira Miller.

An Honest Penny

Deep in the forests of the North there was a woman and her only son. They lived in a hut where the icy wind blew through the cracks in the wall and the cold rain dripped through the leaky roof. They had no money for warm clothes and so little food that they were both as thin as winter twigs.

One morning the woman sent her son out to gather firewood. He ran and slapped his arms and stamped his feet, trying to keep warm as he filled his sack. He bent to pick up a fallen branch. He heard a little sound: a faint

mewing. He moved aside the leaves of a holly
bush and there was a small cat. She looked well
fed but frightened and cold.

'Poor little cat,' said the boy. 'How miserable

you look.' He was not a clever boy but he had a generous nature and, without a second thought, he took off his jacket and wrapped it round the cat. Then, putting his sack on his back, he walked off, whistling.

By the time he reached home, he was shivering and his mother took one look at him and started to shout.

'Are you mad?' she cried angrily. 'Where's your jacket? You will die of cold.'

'Don't be cross,' answered the boy and told her about the little cat.

'That's all very well,' she snapped, 'but now you will freeze. If they have any sense, which you haven't, *everyone puts his own self first*. Go back and get your jacket this instant.'

When the boy reached the holly tree, he bent down and moved the leaves again. There was no sign of the cat and, worse still, no sign of the jacket. What was he to do? As he searched he noticed the corner of an old wooden chest. He dragged it out and opened it. It was full, right to the very top; overflowing with money!

'What's this?' said the boy. 'How could this money have got into the forest?' He knew that so much money would make them rich but he was uneasy in his mind. 'It must be stolen,' he decided. 'Only robbers would bury money in the middle of the forest.' And because he was not a clever boy but had an honest nature, he refused to touch it. He took the chest and emptied it into the lake. The gold and silver flashed and sank to the bottom, except for one single penny which floated on the surface.

'Well,' said the boy, 'that must be an honest penny,' for he knew the superstition which says what is honest will always float. 'I can take that,' he said and returned home, still whistling, without his jacket but clutching just one honest penny.

This time his mother was more than angry. 'You are a fool!' she screamed. 'If you had brought that money home, we could have lived in comfort, eaten the best food and always been warm. Don't you understand? I'm always telling you, *everyone puts his own self first*. Well, I've had enough of you. You can go out and earn your own living.'

And there and then she turned him out and he set off to seek his fortune with just one penny.

At first the boy had no luck. None of the farmers would give him a job. They wanted taller, stronger lads. He walked on, following the river until he reached a sea port where he found work in the house of a rich merchant. He was not a clever boy, as you know, but because he had a generous and honest nature, soon everyone came to like him.

The merchant was preparing for a long voyage to a distant country. As was his custom, before he left, he asked his servants if there was anything he could buy for them. The servants gave the master their money and asked for the goods they wanted. In this way they did a little trading on their own account. The boy had nothing but his penny.

The merchant smiled. 'I don't think I shall get a great deal for one penny,' he said.

'I don't mind,' said the boy, 'buy what you can for it. At least it's an honest penny.'

The merchant, still laughing, promised to do his best and sailed off to the distant land, where he traded his goods for delicately painted bowls, brilliant soft silks and strongly scented spices. Then he took his servants' money and bought what they had asked for. All except for the boy. There was nothing for a penny. Even an honest one.

The merchant stood on the deck, watching the sailors prepare to cast off. As he looked at the busy quay, he saw an old woman with a bag that wriggled and jumped.

'What's in your bag, mother?' he called.

'A fine cat,' she answered. 'You can have her for one penny.'

'Done!' cried the merchant. After all, hadn't the boy said he was to buy what he could with it?

At first the merchant succeeded in keeping the cat in his cabin, but one day the merchant was too slow and the cat shot out of the cabin. It ran up to the top deck and straight up the mainmast, where it sat perfectly still.

'Come down, cat,' shouted the merchant.

The cat stayed where it was, staring down at the merchant. And then it flicked its tail.

The wind began to blow, clouds raced, rain fell and a great storm raged. It raged for three days, driving the ship off course, until calm returned and they found themselves anchored off a port no-one had ever visited before.

The merchant went ashore and walked into an inn. There were many people there and the tables were already laid for dinner. He was welcomed courteously but he could not help wondering why there was a stout stick by each place.

When the food was brought in, he found out. Mice swarmed from every corner of the room and as the people ate, they were obliged to whack the mice that ran all over the table. The merchant was not the only one who broke a plate and whacked his neighbour by mistake.

'This is a miserable business!' cried the merchant. 'Why don't you get a cat?'

'What's a cat?' they asked. In that country no-one had even heard of cats.

The merchant was soon back with the cat in his arms. From that moment they were able to eat in peace.

Before the ship left the townspeople came to ask if they could buy the cat. 'You must leave her with us,' they insisted. 'We will pay anything you ask.'

So the merchant parted with the cat but took instead one hundred sacks of gold.

'A good return for one penny,' thought the merchant as they sailed out of harbour. He glanced upwards. There was the cat, sitting as still as ever, on the top of the mainmast.

'So you managed to get back on board. Good! The boy can have you and I will have the money. After all,' he reasoned, '*everyone puts his own self first.*'

As he spoke, the cat flicked his tail. The storm returned. For three days they ran before the wind, not knowing which direction they sailed in, until they sighted land. As suddenly as before, the storm ceased and they came safely into the strange port.

When the merchant entered the harbour

inn, he saw the tables laid as before. This town seemed prosperous. There was silver cutlery and china plates but by each place was a large iron bar. This time, however, he was alarmed when the arrival of the food was greeted by a swarm of rats. They were large rats. They fought for the food and the merchant ran all the way to the ship to fetch the cat.

In two minutes there were no rats.

'What kind of creature is that?' marvelled the townspeople. 'Name your price. You must leave it with us.'

A thousand bags of gold were loaded on to the ship. As the land disappeared from sight, the merchant went up on deck and looked up the mainmast. There sat the cat.

'Splendid!' said the merchant. 'The boy still has his cat. Perhaps I will give him a coin or two but, after all, I must think of my interests. *Everyone puts his own self first.*'

The cat sat and listened. She made no noise but she flicked her tail.

The wind returned, driving the rain, whipping up the waves until the boat was once more in the grip of a terrible storm. They ran before the wind for three days, then the storm grew worse. They rose and fell, the boat shuddering for day after day. The sailors became terrified.

'She won't last another day,' yelled the captain.

The merchant knew in his heart what he must do. He clung to the mast and shouted up to the cat, 'I give you my word. The boy will get every penny and you, cat, as well. I swear it.'

As he spoke, the storm calmed and soon the ship was sailing home under blue skies with a fair breeze.

The merchant returned to a great welcome. He had traded well both for himself and his servants. The boy was richer than he could understand but delighted with the cat, who greeted him like an old friend. Although he was not a clever boy, he determined to marry the merchant's daughter, which pleased both the daughter and the merchant. His mother was still living in the old hut in the forest so he sent for her and made her comfortable. For, as he said, '*I don't think that everyone should put his own self first.*'

Retelling of a Scandinavian tale by Pat Thomson.

Kamla's Secret

'What are you doing?' asked Kate.

'Oh, nothing,' said Kamla.

'You *were* doing something,' frowned Kate. 'You were twisting your hands in a funny way.'

'That's nothing,' repeated Kamla mysteriously. 'Come on! Let's play!'

The next day at school, while standing in the dinner line, Kate again noticed Kamla twisting her hands and arms. She had a faraway look on her face.

'You're doing it again,' cried Kate.

'Doing what?' asked Kamla.

'Doing this!' And Kate tried to twist her hands and arms as she had seen her friend doing.

Kamla laughed. 'Are you trying to be a snake?'

'No! I'm trying to copy you,' groaned Kate.

Then the line moved on and the dinner ladies served them their meat pie and mashed potatoes and they sat down to eat.

Afterwards, in the playground, Kate said crossly, 'I won't be your friend if you don't tell me what you were doing.'

'I was only trying to think how I could balance a stone on the palm of my hand, and twist my hand round in circles without letting the stone drop off,' explained Kamla.

'That's easy!' cried Kate. She picked up a small stone and tried. But as soon as her palm was twisted halfway round, pointing inwards, the stone fell off.

She tried again and again, but still the stone fell off.

'It's impossible!' she said.

Then Kamla had a go. She put the stone on the flat of her hand and held it outwards. Then slowly she began to twist her palm round in a circle. As her fingers pointed inwards, she tipped her elbow upwards and down again. Her hand stayed flat as it came round, and the stone didn't fall off.

'How do you do it?' gasped Kate, clapping her hands.

'I've been practising,' said Kamla. 'My cousin Leela showed me how. She can do it with a saucer! I think I'll try that when I get home.'

Kate found herself practising too. She couldn't stop trying to do it. She practised and practised until her muscles ached and she felt as if her arm would drop out of its socket. At last she managed it with a stone. She did it in the playground, and was so pleased that she rushed around shouting, 'I've done it! I've done it!'

She showed Miss Evans, the playground supervisor.

'Aren't you clever,' said Miss Evans and she tried too. It was catching!

'Kamla can do it with a saucer now,' said Kate.

'That could work out expensive,' laughed Miss Evans as she dropped the stone.

The next morning the postman called at Kate's house with a large white envelope. Her dad opened it.

'It's an invitation,' he said. 'We're all invited to a Diwali party at the Guptas next Saturday evening.'

'What's Diwali?' asked Kate's mum.

'It's a Festival of Light, according to one of my mates at work,' said her dad. 'He mentioned it the other day. It should be interesting.'

Kate was very excited. She had never been to an evening party before with grown-ups.

'We're all coming to your party next Saturday,' she told Kamla when she got to school.

'Oh good,' said Kamla. She seemed very excited too, but also a bit secretive.

'We're preparing a lot of surprises for you,' she whispered darkly.

At last Saturday came round. It was a dull, rainy day. Kate looked gloomily out of the window. How was she going to pass the hours?

'Mum, can I put on my party dress now?' she asked.

'No, dear,' replied her mother. 'It's only nine o'clock in the morning and the party isn't until seven tonight!'

Kate sighed with boredom. Kamla couldn't come round and play because she was helping to prepare the Diwali party.

'Can't I help too?' Kate had asked.

'Oh, no!' cried Kamla. 'You'd find out all the surprises!'

Kate decided to try balancing a saucer on her hand and twisting it round. She twisted carefully . . . up . . . round . . . in . . . and CRASH! The saucer slipped from her palm and smashed on the floor.

'What are you doing?' cried her mother, rushing in.

'I was practising,' said Kate glumly.

'Not with my saucers, you don't,' retorted her mother. 'Come on, I think you'd better go shopping with Daddy before you get up to any more mischief!'

And so the hours dragged by. But at last darkness fell, and her mother suddenly said, 'Come on, Kate! It's time to get ready for the party!'

Kate whooped with joy and rushed upstairs.

There, lying on her bed, was her long, green and white party dress with frilly sleeves and a green, velvet sash.

Her mother dressed up too in her prettiest skirt and blouse, and her father wore a tie; something he hardly ever did except for weddings and funerals! Then they all set off.

It was no longer raining. The night sky had cleared and was spangled with stars. Then they saw the first surprise.

'Look! Look at Kamla's house!' squealed Kate. 'It's all lit up!'

'They're real flames!' exclaimed Mum.

As they drew nearer they could see that every window sill was lined with small saucers of glowing lights. Even the garden path was lined with flickering flames from wicks dipped in oil.

The front door flew open and Kamla came skipping out. She was wearing her Indian costume, the pink, satin pyjamas and tunic which her cousin Leela had brought her from India.

'Hello! Hello! Come in!' she called

excitedly, and she grabbed Kate's hand and pulled her inside.

'Welcome to our Diwali celebrations,' said Kamla's mother and father. Kamla's mother looked very beautiful in a purple and gold saree, while Mr Gupta wore special wrinkly, white trousers and a black, silk jacket buttoned up to the neck.

'I'm so glad you could come,' he said, and led them into the living room.

The room was already full of friends and neighbours, all dressed up in their party clothes.

Instead of putting on the electric lights, there were little dishes of oil and wicks flickering in every niche and on the mantelpiece. The light from them made the gold and silver threads in the sarees glisten; it made the sequins and beads on Kamla's costume flash and sparkle; it made the jewels in the necklaces and earrings gleam brightly, and it made the shadows on the walls tremble darkly.

Leela passed among the guests carrying trays of drinks and Indian titbits to nibble.

In the dining room the table was piled high with all sorts of delicious food. Plates of chappatis and purees, dishes of chutneys and pickles, great bowls of steaming fluffy rice and rich, red curry and several plates full of different kinds of Indian sweets.

'What a feast!' breathed Kate's dad in amazement.

After everyone had eaten and mingled and chatted, Mr Gupta clapped his hands.

'Now we have some entertainment for you!'

Everyone sat down excitedly on the chairs and sofas and on the floor, leaving a circle in the middle.

Mr Gupta brought out his accordion and Mrs Gupta held two small, brass bells like tiny cymbals, one in each hand.

There was a jangling of ankle bells, and Leela stepped into the middle of the circle. Everyone clapped with delight. She was wearing an Indian dance costume of scarlet and gold. Her bare feet and hands were painted red, and her eyes were outlined in black to make them look larger.

She stamped her jangly feet and Kamla's mother and father began to play. The dance started slowly as Leela twisted her hands and flashed her eyes. Gradually the beat got faster and faster and soon she was spinning round like a brightly coloured top with her costume whirling round her.

The dance ended with a flourish. Everybody cheered and clapped. Kate looked round for Kamla, but she was nowhere to be seen.

'I can't see Kamla!' Kate whispered.

'Shh!' nudged her mother. 'Mrs Gupta is going to sing.'

When the song was over, Kate suddenly caught sight of her friend. This was a really big surprise. Kamla was dressed up as a dancing girl too. Her eyes were outlined in black; she had a red mark in the middle of her forehead, and the palms of her hands were painted red too. There were jangling bells round her ankles and glass bangles tinkled on her wrists.

'Mummy! Look at Kamla!' cried Kate in astonishment.

Everyone looked surprised. Even Kamla's mother and father.

'Kamla has been secretly learning a very special dance for Diwali,' announced Leela, leading her little cousin into the centre of the circle.

There was a rustle of excitement. Kamla's mother beamed with pleasure.

'Kamla will now dance a temple dance in which she offers a gift of light to the god.' Then Leela stepped over to the mantelpiece and took down a very small saucer with a softly burning light. She placed it on the palm of Kamla's outstretched hand.

'So that's what she was practising so secretly,' hissed Kate. 'I hope she doesn't drop it!'

First Kamla stood like a statue with the flame burning in her hand. Then, as the accordion breathed out its tune, and the bells clashed a rhythm, she stamped first one foot then the other. Gradually she began to move round, gliding gracefully so as not to upset the saucer of flame. She swayed this way and that, raising the saucer from one side to the other.

Then came the really hard bit. Kate could hardly bear to look. Kamla began to twist her palm round as she had done in the playground. Would she drop the saucer? Would she get burnt by the flame as it twisted under? No-one dared make a sound.

Kamla twisted the saucer on her palm round . . . and round . . . and round . . . while she gradually dropped lower and lower to the ground. At last she was kneeling and brought the saucer in its last circle down to the ground. She placed it like an offering in the middle of the room.

Everyone burst out cheering and clapping.

'Shabash!' they shouted. 'Well done!' What a secret! Kate didn't know, and not even Kamla's mother had known!

Leela was very proud of her pupil. 'I wanted to teach her an Indian dance before I went home,' she said.

Kamla jingled and jangled as she jumped up and down enjoying all the praise.

'I love dancing,' she cried. 'I wish Leela

wasn't going home because there'll be no-one to teach me.'

'Why don't you come to my ballet class?' suggested Kate.

'What do you do?' asked Kamla, interested.

'Well, you don't wear bells round your ankles or carry saucers. Instead of stamping you run on tiptoe and point your toes – in ballet shoes of course!'

'Don't you dress up?' asked Kamla, whirling her costume. 'I do love dressing up!'

'Only at Christmas, then sometimes we wear tu-tus like real ballerinas!'

'I think you should go with Kate to her ballet classes,' said Leela. 'Then, when you come and visit me in India one day you can entertain us with ballet dancing!'

'Can I come too?' begged Kate.

'Who knows!' laughed Leela. 'Who knows!'

At last the party was over. Everyone thanked Mr and Mrs Gupta, and they thanked Leela and Kamla. Then they went out into the night.

It was just beginning to rain a little and the

flames in the saucers began to splutter and go out.

'Could we have a party like that?' asked Kate as they hurried home. 'Then I could dance in my tu-tu for everyone.'

'Let's have a party on Bonfire night,' suggested Dad. 'It's Guy Fawkes night in a week or two.'

'I can't promise a feast like the Guptas gave,' laughed Mum, 'but I think I could manage some baked potatoes and sausages, and mugs of hot chocolate.'

'Yes,' agreed Kate enthusiastically. 'That would be fun. We must send out invitations immediately.'

'Please try and wait till tomorrow,' begged her mother. 'It is nearly midnight.'

'Oh all right!' agreed Kate, and hurried off to bed to dream of bonfires and fireworks and dancing with saucers of flame.

This story is by Jamila Gavin.

The Froggy Princess

A long time ago, when there were dragons and wicked witches and knights in armour and fairy tales were true, there lived a beautiful princess called Princess Amanda.

I said she was beautiful. Well, she was beautiful when she wasn't crying. But she was always crying. Her nose was always red from crying, and her eyes were puffy and pink from crying.

Why did she cry so much? Because she was waiting for a handsome Prince to come to the castle and marry her. But no Prince ever came. Not one.

One fine summer day, Princess Amanda cried harder than she had ever cried before. She wept *buckets*. She cried so much and for so long that the tall, narrow turret in which she lived began to fill with water. It was when the water had risen just above her knees that she saw the frog. The frog was swimming in the water with its back legs going Per-chung, Per-chung. Its bright round eyes stared straight at her.

'Go away!' said the Princess. 'I hate frogs! All slippery and slimy! Ugh!'

The frog said, 'Qu-arckk.' Then, 'Don't be rude.'

'What did you say?' said Princess Amanda who was so surprised by the talking frog that she forgot to cry. '*What?*'

The frog hopped out of the water and into the Princess's lap.

It was then that the Princess noticed the frog was wearing a nice little gold crown. 'Gracious me!' she said. 'You're a Fairy-Tale Frog!'

'Quite right,' said the frog in its croaky voice. 'Really, I'm a handsome Prince. But a wicked witch cast a magic spell and turned me into a frog.'

'Oh, how sad,' said Princess Amanda, weeping more than ever.

'If a Princess kisses me,' the frog said, 'I'll turn back into a handsome Prince, with a sword at my side and a curly feather in my hat. You are a Princess, aren't you? Just one little kiss . . .'

'Kiss *you*?' said Princess Amanda. 'Never!'

'We'll be married and live happily ever after,' said the frog.

'Kiss a slimy, slippery *frog*?' said Princess Amanda. She sounded disgusted. But she was thinking he really is a very handsome frog, and he should turn out to be a very handsome Prince.

So she bent down, pulled a face and kissed the frog.

WHAM! BANG! WALLOP! BOOM! There was thunder and lightning and drums and trumpets — and ABRACADABRA! The

spell cast by the Wicked Witch was ended!

The trouble was that the spell ended the wrong way.

Instead of the frog turning into a Prince, the Princess turned into a frog. Yes, a girl frog, with a yellow tummy, green spots and stripes, and a little gold crown with pearls round the edge.

At first, Princess Amanda was furious. But soon she began to cheer up. She soon learned hopping, jumping and swimming – it was good fun. Being damp and watery did not bother her. She had spent all her life crying, so she was used to the wet. Best of all, her frog Prince was, to her eyes, very handsome indeed. And very popular. All the frogs cheered like anything when Princess Amanda became the Prince's bride. The underwater wedding was splendid.

Time passed and the couple had many royal children, some striped, some spotted and some a bit of both. So Princess Amanda gave up crying and, indeed, lived happily ever after.

Now, all this took place a long time ago. But even today, when you meet a frog – be careful. You should treat every frog with respectful politeness. Because, you see, your frog could be a royal frog; one of the great, great, great, great grandchildren of Princess Amanda.

This story is by Nicholas Fisk.

The Quarrel

As soon as Ramona stepped through the back door, she knew something was wrong. There was a chill about the house, and it had the faint mustiness of a place that had been closed and unoccupied all day. There was no welcoming fragrance of simmering meat and vegetables. The tiny light on the Crock-Pot was dark, the pot cold.

'Oh, no!' cried Mrs Quimby, noticing.

'What's wrong?' asked Mr Quimby, coming in from the hall where he had gone to turn up the thermostat of the furnace.

'Wrong!' Mrs Quimby lifted the lid of the electric casserole on the kitchen counter. 'Someone forgot to plug in the Crock-Pot this morning, that's what's wrong.'

The family gathered to peer in at the cold vegetables and raw meat.

'I'm starving!' wailed Beezus.

'Me, too,' said Ramona.

'I thought you turned it on,' said Mrs

Quimby to her husband as she shoved the plug into the socket. The stew could cook overnight and be warmed up for the next evening.

'Don't look at me,' said Mr Quimby to his wife. 'I thought you turned it on.' There was an edge to his voice.

For some reason his remark annoyed Mrs Quimby. 'I suppose you think turning on a Crock-Pot is woman's work.' The edge in her voice matched the edge in his.

'Not exactly,' said Mr Quimby, 'but now that you mention it—'

'Don't forget the time you forgot to fork the potatoes you put in to bake and they exploded,' his wife reminded him.

Ramona stifled a laugh at that memory. Her father had looked so surprised the evening the potatoes exploded – *poof!* – when he had opened the oven door.

Mr Quimby was not going to be drawn into a discussion of past baked potatoes. 'Why not just throw the stuff into the frying pan and cook it?' he asked. His idea of cooking was to toss everything into a pan and stir until done. Sometimes he invented interesting dishes with ground meat and eggs, zucchini and cheese. Other times the family tried to be good sports at dinner.

'Because you can't fry stewing meat.' Mrs Quimby sounded annoyed as she looked into the cupboard and the refrigerator. 'It's too tough. You know that. Did you bring groceries?'

'No. I thought we were having stew for dinner,' answered Mr Quimby. Crossly, Ramona thought. 'I didn't see anything on the grocery list.'

Picky-picky, the cat, rubbed against Mrs Quimby's legs, telling her how hungry he was. 'Scat,' said Mrs Quimby.

Picky-picky went to Beezus, not Ramona. He did not like Ramona, had never liked her because she was too noisy.

'I'm practically dying of hunger,' said Beezus as she picked up the old cat and rubbed her cheek against him.

'Me, too,' said Ramona.

70

'You girls are no help,' Mrs Quimby told her daughters. 'We have a couple of eggs, not enough for an omelet, two strips of bacon, three carrots, and some tired old lettuce. That's it.' She looked at her husband. 'We don't have to let the cupboard get completely bare before we buy groceries.'

This remark gave Ramona a cue. 'Old Mother Hubbard went to the cupboard—' she began, but she did not finish the rhyme because she could see no-one was listening.

'Anytime we are low on groceries, just make a list,' said Mr Quimby. 'That's all you have to do.'

'I could make carrot salad,' suggested Beezus, as if carrot salad might smooth things over.

'We could have pancakes,' said Mr Quimby, 'with half a strip of bacon apiece.'

'Not a very nutritious meal,' said Mrs Quimby, 'but better than starvation.' She reached for a mixing bowl while Beezus, who had dropped Picky-picky and washed her hands, began to grate carrots onto a sheet of waxed paper. Ramona leaned against the counter to watch. She wanted to make sure her sister did not grate her fingers into the salad.

'Ramona, don't just stand there,' said Mr Quimby as he laid the bacon in a frying pan. 'Get busy and set the table. As my grandmother used to say, "Every kettle must rest on its own bottom," so do your part.'

Ramona made a face as she reached for the place mats. 'Daddy, I bet your grandmother didn't really say all the things you say she said.'

'If she did, she must have been a dreadful bore,' said Mrs Quimby, who was beating batter as if she were angry with it.

Mr Quimby looked hurt. 'You didn't know my grandmother.'

'If she went around spouting wisdom all the time, I can't say I'm sorry.' Mrs Quimby was on her knees, dragging the griddle from behind the pots and pans in the bottom of the cupboard.

Ramona paused in laying the silverware to make sure there was no blood on the carrots.

She felt the muscles of her stomach tighten as they always tightened when her mother was cross with her father.

'My grandmother was a wonderful woman,' said Mr Quimby. 'She had a hard life out there in the country, but she was good to us kids and we learned a lot from her.'

'Well, my grandmother wasn't so bad herself.' With an angry sounding crash the griddle knocked over two pans and a double boiler as Mrs Quimby yanked it from the cupboard. 'And I learned a lot from her.'

Ramona and Beezus exchanged an anxious look.

'Just what did you learn from your grandmother?' asked Mr Quimby. 'As far as I could see, all she ever did was gad around and play bridge.'

Ramona and Beezus exchanged another look. Were their parents quarrelling? Really quarrelling? Yes, the sisters' eyes agreed. Both girls were worried.

Mrs Quimby set the griddle on the stove with more noise than necessary. She was plainly trying to think what she had learned from her grandmother. Finally she said, 'My grandmother taught me to pick flowers with long stems and to pick a few leaves to put in with them.'

'Very useful,' said Mr Quimby.

The hint of sarcasm in his voice must have annoyed Mrs Quimby because she said, 'My grandmother didn't have much money, but she had a sense of beauty.' The drop of water she flicked on the griddle refused to dance.

'No matter how much my grandmother had to scrimp and pinch to make ends meet,' said Mr Quimby, 'she always managed to find money to buy paper for me to draw on.'

Scrimp and pinch to make ends meet, thought Ramona, liking the sound of the words. She would remember them. The smell of bacon sizzling made her feel better. It also made her hungrier.

'My grandmother taught me useful things, too.' Mrs Quimby had had time to think. 'She taught me that a dab of spit would stop a run in a stocking.' She flicked another drop of water on the griddle. This one danced. The griddle was hot.

'Some grandmother,' said Mr Quimby, 'spitting on her stockings.'

'You're both being silly,' Beezus burst out. 'Just plain silly!'

'Young lady, you keep out of this,' ordered Mr Quimby.

Beezus glared at her father. 'Well, you are,' she muttered.

Mrs Quimby silently poured four puddles of batter on the griddle. Ramona prayed that the quarrel, whatever it was about, was over.

Beezus stirred mayonnaise into the blood-free carrots, which she then divided on four limp lettuce leaves on four salad plates. Mr Quimby turned the bacon. Mrs Quimby flipped the pancakes. Ramona's stomach relaxed. In a moment her mother would slide the pancakes onto a platter and start another four cooking. Ramona could hardly wait, she was so hungry.

'Are you sure those pancakes are done?' asked Mr Quimby as his wife slid the pancake turner under them. 'They don't look done to me.'

'They bubbled in the middle before I turned them,' said Mrs Quimby, 'and they look done to me.'

Mr Quimby took the pancake turner from his wife. Using it as a weapon, he slashed each pancake in the centre. Ramona and Beezus exchanged a shocked look. Their father had slashed their mother's pancakes! He had gone too far. Frightened, they watched raw batter ooze from four gashes in the pancakes. Their father was right. The cakes were not done. Now what would their mother do?

Mrs Quimby was furious. She snatched back the pancake turner, scooped up the oozing cakes, and tossed them into the garbage.

'You didn't need to do that.' Mr Quimby looked amused. He had won. 'You could have turned them again and let them finish cooking.'

'And I suppose your grandmother made absolutely perfect pancakes,' said Mrs Quimby in a voice stiff with anger.

Mr Quimby looked calm and even more amused. 'As a matter of fact, she did,' he said. 'Brown and lacy, cooked all the way through, and with crisp edges.'

'The best pancakes you ever ate,' stated Mrs Quimby in a voice that made Ramona silently pray. Mother, be nice again. Please, please be nice again.

'Right,' said Mr Quimby. 'Light enough to melt in your mouth.'

Be quiet, Daddy, prayed Ramona. You'll make things worse.

'Oh – you!' Mrs Quimby gave Mr Quimby

a swat on the seat of his pants with the pancake turner before she threw it on the counter. 'Bake them yourself since you learned so much from that noble grand-mother of yours!'

Ramona and Beezus stood frozen with shock. Their mother had hit their father with a pancake turner. Ramona wanted to fly at her mother, to strike her and cry out, You hit my daddy! She dared not.

Mr Quimby tucked a dish towel in his belt for an apron and calmly ladled batter onto the griddle while his wife stalked into the living room and sat down with the newspaper. If only he wouldn't whistle so cheerfully as he deftly turned the cakes and drained the bacon.

'Dinner is served,' Mr Quimby announced as he set a platter of hot cakes and bacon on the table and pulled the dish towel from his belt. Silently Mrs Quimby joined the family.

Even though her mother was usually a much better cook than her father, Ramona had to admit her father made excellent pancakes. Unfortunately, she was no longer very hungry. She felt all churned up inside, as if she didn't know whether to cry or to burst out of the house shouting, My mother and father had a fight!

'Please pass the butter.' Mrs Quimby might have been speaking to a stranger.

'May I please have the syrup?' Mr Quimby asked politely.

'The funniest thing happened at school,' said Beezus, and Ramona understood that her sister was anxious to start a conversation that would smooth things over and make their parents forget their quarrel, perhaps make them laugh.

After a moment of silence Mrs Quimby said, 'Tell me.'

'You'll never guess how a boy spelled *relief* in a spelling test,' said Beezus.

'How?' asked Ramona to help the conversation along. Mr Quimby silently served himself two more hot cakes.

'He spelled it *r-o-l-a-i-d-s*,' said Beezus, looking anxiously at her parents, who actually smiled.

Ramona did not smile. 'But the man on television spells *relief* that way. He said r–*o-l-a-i-d-s* spells *relief*. I've heard him.'

'Silly,' said Beezus, but this time she spoke with affection. 'That's just a slogan. *Relief* is *r-e-l-i-e-f*.'

'Oh.' Ramona was glad to know. Table–talk sank back into silence while Ramona thought about spelling. Spelling was full of traps – bends and silent letters and letters that sounded one way in one word and a different way in another – and having a man stand there on television fooling children was no help. She was glad she had a big sister who understood those things.

The evening was quiet. Mr Quimby dozed in front of the television set. Mrs Quimby took a shower and went to bed to read. Beezus did her homework in her room. Ramona tried to draw a monster eating a mouthful of people, but she could not make the picture on paper match the one in her imagination. Her monster looked as if he were eating paper dolls instead of real people. The house was

unnaturally quiet. The television droned on.
Both girls went to bed without being told.

Unhappy thoughts kept Ramona awake.
What if her mother and father did not love
one another any more? What if they decided
to get a divorce like her friend Davy's parents?
What would happen to her? Who would take
care of her? Beezus was closer to being a
grown-up, but what about Ramona? She
wanted to cry but could not. She felt too tight
inside to cry. Tears teetered on her eyelashes
but would not give her the relief of falling.

81

Finally Ramona could stand her fear and loneliness no longer. She slipped out of bed and tiptoed into her sister's room.

'Ramona?' Beezus too was awake.

'I can't go to sleep,' whispered Ramona.

'Neither can I,' said Beezus. 'Come on, get in bed with me.'

This invitation was what Ramona had been hoping for. Gratefully she slipped beneath the covers and snuggled against her sister. 'Do you think they'll get a divorce?' she whispered. 'They won't talk to each other.'

'Of course not,' said Beezus. 'At least I don't think so.'

'Who would take care of me if they did?' Ramona felt she had to have the answer from someone. 'I'm still little.' Beezus, of course, was her mother's girl, but what about Ramona?

Beezus seemed to be considering the question. 'I'll try,' she said at last.

'You aren't grown up enough,' said Ramona, nevertheless comforted. Beezus cared.

'I know,' admitted Beezus. 'I read a book

about a girl who took care of her brothers and sisters when their father died, but that was off in the mountains someplace where they all picked herbs and things. It wouldn't work in the city.'

'Mother and Daddy won't be dead.' Ramona was consoled by this knowledge.

Beezus was silent awhile. 'They could have been joking,' she said. 'Sort of.'

'But Mother hit Daddy,' Ramona pointed out. 'On the seat of his pants with a pancake turner.'

'I don't think that's the same as if she had hit him with something hard,' said Beezus. 'After all, she didn't really hurt him.'

Ramona tried to find a bright side. 'And he didn't hit her back,' she said. 'But if they loved us, they wouldn't fight.' She silently said her prayers, ending with, 'Please, please don't let Mother and Daddy fight.'

From the kitchen came a whiff of the stew that would simmer through the night for their supper the next evening. Soothed by the homey fragrance, the sisters fell asleep.

In the morning, a few seconds after she awoke and found herself in her sister's bed, a dull, unhappy feeling settled over Ramona. Her parents had quarrelled. She dreaded facing them at breakfast. She did not know what to say to them. Beezus looked unhappy, too. Getting dressed took longer than usual, and when they finally went into the kitchen, they were surprised to see their parents sharing the morning paper as they ate breakfast together.

'Good morning, girls,' said Mr Quimby with his usual cheerfulness.

'There is oatmeal on the stove.' Mrs Quimby smiled fondly at her daughters. 'Did you sleep well?'

Beezus was suddenly angry. 'No, we didn't!'

'No, we didn't,' echoed Ramona, encouraged by her sister's anger. How could her mother expect them to sleep well when they were so worried?

Startled, both parents laid down the newspaper.

'And it's all your fault,' Beezus informed them.

'What on earth are you talking about?' asked Mrs Quimby.

Beezus was near tears. 'Your big fight, that's what.'

Ramona blinked back tears, too. 'You wouldn't even talk to each other. And you hit Daddy!'

'Of course we were speaking,' said Mrs Quimby. 'Where did you get the idea we weren't? We were just tired is all. We had one of those days when everything seemed to go wrong.'

So did I, thought Ramona.

'I went to bed and read,' continued Mrs Quimby, 'and your father watched television. That was all there was to it.'

Ramona felt almost limp with relief. At the same time she was angry with her parents for causing so much worry. 'Grown-ups aren't supposed to fight,' she informed them.

'Oh, for heaven's sake,' said Mrs Quimby. 'Why not?'

Ramona was stern. 'Grown-ups are supposed to be perfect.'

Both her parents laughed. 'Well, they are,' Ramona insisted, annoyed by their laughter.

'Name one perfect grown-up,' challenged Mr Quimby. 'You can't do it.'

'Haven't you noticed grown-ups aren't perfect?' asked Mrs Quimby. 'Especially when they're tired.'

'Then how come you expect us kids to be so perfect all the time?' demanded Ramona.

'Good question,' said Mr Quimby. 'I'll have to think of an answer.'

'We want you to be perfect so you won't grow up to bicker about your grandmothers and their pancakes,' said Mrs Quimby. Both parents thought her reply was funny.

Ramona felt the way Picky-picky looked when someone rumpled his fur. Maybe grown-ups weren't perfect, but they should be, her parents most of all. They should be cheerful, patient, loving, never sick and never tired. And fun, too.

'You kids fight,' said Mr Quimby. 'Why shouldn't we?'

'It isn't dignified,' said Beezus, giving Ramona another word to add to her list. 'Especially when you hit someone with a pancake turner.'

'Oh, you silly little girls,' said Mrs Quimby with amusement and affection.

'Why should we let you kids have all the fun?' asked Mr Quimby.

'We don't quarrel for fun,' Ramona informed her father.

'You could fool me,' said Mr Quimby.

Ramona refused to smile. 'Don't you ever do it again,' she ordered her parents in her sternest voice.

'Yes, ma'am,' answered Mrs Quimby with mock meekness, as if she were poking a little fun at Ramona.

'Yes, *ma'am*!' said her father, and saluted as if she were somebody important.

This time Ramona had to laugh.

This story is by Beverly Cleary.

The Giant Who Wanted to Eat Boys

A time came when there was only one giant left in the world.

This giant lived in a castle on top of a high hill; a green moss-covered castle full of empty rooms where only the giant spiders moved as they spun their everlasting webs and cut out the sunlight.

Some days the giant sat still and did nothing from morning to night, but there were days when he walked about his castle. When he did this:

the earth shook, the trees clashed
the rocks danced, the streams dashed,

and the people who lived in the valley below looked up and said, 'The Old Giant is walking about upstairs!' and they laughed and went on with what they were doing.

The village baker didn't laugh though. He was a thoughtful man. He'd pause in his work, and look at his dough, and shake his head and say, 'So long as he doesn't walk this way!' But nobody took any notice of him.

Sometimes the giant sang to himself. He

could only remember one song — a nursery-rhyme for baby giants, so he always sang that:

'Hot Cross Boys, Hot Cross Boys.
One-a-penny, two-a-penny,
HOT CROSS BOYS.'

He sang very loudly and stamped his great feet to the time, till the earth shook,

the trees clashed and clashed
the rocks danced and danced
the streams dashed and dashed,

and the people who lived in the valley below looked up and said, 'That's the Old Giant making a noise upstairs!' and they laughed and went on with what they were doing.

The people who lived in the valley knew about the giant, but as the giant knew nothing about them they felt very safe.

'He might find out one day and then what?' the baker would say to himself as he banged and battered the dough.

Now, the only food the giant had to eat was bread-and-cheese or cheese-and-bread. Nothing more. He got very tired of that.

So, before he sat down to a meal he'd cheer himself up with his song:

'Hot Cross Boys, Hot Cross Boys.
Be they fatter, be they thinner,
They will make a tasty dinner:
HOT CROSS BOYS!'

As he picked up his piece of coarse brown bread and bit into his lump of hard yellow cheese, he'd sigh and say: 'Oh, I wonder what boys *are*? I wonder what they taste like? THEY DO SOUND NICE.'

Then, one day when the giant was walking about his castle and annoying the giant spiders by breaking their webs as he did so, he tripped over something that was lying on the floor among the cobwebs. 'Ho-ho,' he said. 'What's this?'

He bent down and picked it up. It was a dirty metal tube with a filthy piece of glass at each end of it.

'Why, it's a spy-glass!' cried the giant. 'I'd forgotten there were such things! I can have fun with this!'

He cleaned the pipe on his sleeve and polished the glass at each end with his tie.

'What do I do now?' he thought. 'It's so long ago since I held a spy-glass in my hands.'

At last he put it to his eye and looked through the big end straight at one of the giant spiders, and the giant spider seemed very small up there on its web: no more than a speck, he could hardly see it.

'Oh-ho,' said the giant, 'that's a funny thing!' He turned the spy-glass round and looked through the small end and there was the giant spider waving his legs in anger, and the giant spider looked enormous – big as a giant elephant, frightening as a giant octopus!

'Ugh,' said the giant, 'I don't think much of you! I'll take a look out of the window and see if there is anything better to see outside.'

And he beat and brushed away the cobwebs that covered the window, opened it, and leaned out with his spy-glass to his eye and looked down on to the valley below, at the green fields and red-roofed houses of the village.

He twiddled and twisted the spy-glass till the houses looked bigger and BIGGER. Then he saw PEOPLE. People working, walking, running, talking and going about their daily affairs never dreaming that they were being watched.

The giant fiddled with the spy-glass, turning it more and more until the people looked HUGE.

'Giants!' bellowed the giant. 'So I'm not the only one! And they were there all the time! How happy they look and how well fed they appear to be. I don't suppose they have to live on bread-and-cheese as I do. I expect they have Hot Cross Boys whenever they fancy them.'

He thought very hard: 'I'm sure they do!'

He thought harder still. 'I know what I'll do, I'll go and ask if they could spare me some.'

He laughed out loud, and dropping the spy-glass he went out of the castle and down to the valley below, singing as he went:

'Hot Cross Boys, Hot Cross Boys!
Bite them, crunch them,
Chew and munch them –
HOT CROSS BOYS!'

And as he went down the earth cracked, the trees fell, the rocks rolled and the streams over-flowed and everything tumbled and gushed to the valley.

'The giant is coming! The giant is coming!' the people cried, and they dropped everything they were doing and ran away to find somewhere to hide.

'What shall we do? What shall we do?' they wailed as they clambered into lofts or buried themselves in straw-heaps.

'We'll have to wait and see what he's after,' said the baker, putting aside his dough and going off to hide in a flour-bin. But he left it open at the top so that he could peep at the giant.

When the giant arrived at the village there was no-one in sight, and all he could see were the little houses around his feet.

'Where have the giants gone?' he said sadly. 'Who is there to offer me a dish of Hot Cross Boys?'

And he began to cry. Enormous sobs shook him, and great tears ran down his face and fell in puddles or splashed on the roofs below.

The people, hearing the giant crying and the sound of tears pattering on their roofs, crept out of hiding and peeped round corners at him.

The tear-puddles grew larger and larger. Soon they joined and became one puddle and then they began to flow down the street. 'He will flood our houses,' they whispered to one another. 'What is wrong with him? We must do something to stop him weeping like this.'

But nobody offered to confront the giant.

Until at last the baker, who all this time had been peeping from his flour-bin and thinking hard, crept out from hiding, and began to dust some of the flour from his clothes, saying:

'I'll speak to him. But it's no use saying anything from down here. I will go into the church – it's our highest building, and if someone will give me a leg-up, I'll climb to the top of the steeple. If I shout he should hear me from there.'

And that's just what happened.

Suddenly, in the middle of his weeping, the giant heard a little shout: 'Do you want any help, sir?' it said.

The giant looked downwards and saw a tiny floury man clinging to the church steeple. The steeple came just up to his knee, so he bent his head to see and hear better. 'I hoped I would find some giants,' he said sadly. 'I – I hoped they would ask me to dinner!

'All I have in my green-mossy castle is bread-and-cheese and I'm so tired of that.'

He spoke in such a mournful voice that the people came right out from their hiding places and stood in the open to stare. The giant looked at them in amazement, then, seeing they seemed afraid of him, he said kindly, 'I only wanted some boys to eat. I've never tasted boys.' And to show them what he meant he began to sing:

'Hot Cross Boys, Hot Cross Boys!
One-a-penny, two-a-penny,
HOT CROSS BOYS.'

He'd hardly opened his mouth to sing, when all the boys of the village took to their heels and sped away in all directions, and all the villagers shrieked.

The giant stopped singing. 'Why did they do that?' he asked.

'They are BOYS. They don't want you to eat them,' said the baker sternly.

'Oh dear,' said the giant. 'I didn't know boys were like that. They will be hard to catch, and very wriggly to eat. Still, I understand they make a *very tasty dinner*!'

When he said that, the people fell on their knees and pleaded: 'Please don't eat our boys.'

'Surely you can spare me one or two,' said the giant. 'Surely you don't want to keep all those hot cross boys for yourselves?'

The people were silent with horror. Only the baker spoke – or rather, shouted. 'You can have all the Hot Cross Boys you like, sir,' he yelled politely, and the people groaned.

'He doesn't want our boys,' cried the quick-witted baker. 'He wants HOT CROSS BOYS, and I'm the man to make them.

'Just sit down in that field over there, sir,' he called to the giant, 'and I will make you some right away.'

So the giant went to the field and sat down on a haystack while the baker slid down from the church steeple and hurried off to his bake-house.

He mixed some dough. He rolled it flat. Then, he took up his knife and he cut out lots and lots of bun-boys: big ones and small ones – fat ones and thin ones! He stuck in currant eyes and cherry noses and bits of peel-turned-down-at-the-corners for mouths. Then he put them into the oven to bake.

When they were ready he took them out to the giant. They were very, very hot and with all their mouths turned down they looked very, very cross.

'There!' said the clever baker, 'HOT CROSS BOYS!'

'They *do* look good,' said the happy giant, and he settled himself on the haystack and ate and ate and ate.

The baker made more and more and more Hot Cross Boys and all the people ran backwards and forwards carrying the trays of Hot Cross Bun-Boys to the hungry giant.

It was almost nightfall when at last the giant said, 'I'm full up!'

He got up very slowly, because he was so full, and he said, 'Isn't it funny? Now I've eaten so many Hot Cross Boys, I don't think I'll want to taste any more as long as I live. There's a lot to be said for cheese-and-bread!'

And back he went to his castle, slowly and carefully because he was so full, so slowly and carefully that not a tree trembled, not a rock quivered, not a stream rippled, while in the valley the people cheered from relief.

And after that the giant never sang again, although he often looked out of his castle window and watched the people through his spy-glass.

As for the clever baker, he made many bun-boys after that. But he put the peel for their mouths with the corners turning up.

He called them HOT SMILING BOYS and they were so good they sold like hot cakes!

This story is by Dorothy Edwards.

The Hurricane Tree

Once upon a time there was a boy called William, who lived in an old house underneath a tall tree.

In the spring the tree was like a big pale green umbrella, higher than the rooftop, and if William looked up into the branches, he could see birds building their nests.

In the summer, he had his lunch under the tree, then leaned on its smooth warm trunk and fed the crumbs to the squirrels.

In the autumn, the tree dropped sticky prickly beech-nuts into William's sandpit, and

threw down heaps of dry golden leaves. He made beds out of them, and mountains, and kicked them into snowstorms.

And in the winter, when the real snow came, his mummy sometimes took him to the kitchen window at bedtime, to see the big yellow moon through the top of the tree. 'It looks like a balloon tangled up in the branches,' said William. 'One day, when I'm big, I'm going to climb right up that tree and sit next to a bird's nest and look at the stars.'

'It's a very old tree,' said William's daddy. 'It's more than a hundred years old. Someone must have planted it in the old days, and looked after it to help it grow straight and strong.'

'What was it like in the old days?' said William.

'Well,' said his daddy, 'I wasn't even born then, so I don't remember. But when that tree was a new shoot, there weren't any cars, or aeroplanes, or tractors. Big brown horses worked on the land instead, pulling ploughs and carts. And the people didn't have electricity, either. They cooked their food on wood fires.'

'Just like a barbecue,' said William.

'They didn't have electric lights, either,' said his mummy. 'The children had candles to light them to bed.'

But one night, very late, William woke up feeling a bit frightened. A wind was blowing outside, a very strong wind indeed. He could hear the tiles rattling on the roof, and the trees sighing and creaking. The noise made him sad. He climbed out of bed and went to the window, but everything was black outside, because there was no moon. He couldn't see the garden, and he couldn't see the tree. Something went CRASH! in the dark, and his little sister Lucy started to cry in her sleep. William had to keep his eyes shut, so he didn't cry too.

Suddenly his daddy came in with a torch in his hand, making big black shadows on the wall. 'The electricity isn't working. I think the wind must have blown the wires down. But we can see all right with the torch. You two can come into bed with Mummy and me.'

William tried to sleep in the big bed, but the wind was still howling around the house and whistling in the chimney-pots, and he kept thinking about the birds in the tall tree branches. 'Will they be all right in the wind?' he asked. But his mummy and daddy were asleep. Once he thought he heard a cracking sound, and a sigh, out in the garden. Then he went to sleep too.

In the morning, the family came downstairs and looked out of the window. 'Oh!' they all shouted together. The big beech tree was down. The wind had knocked it right over in the night. You could see its roots tipped up against the sky, and even the very top branches were lying on the ground, in the mud by the garden gate. And all the secret shadows had gone from the garden.

William began to cry. 'You said it took a hundred years to grow that tree!' he sobbed. 'But people don't live as long as that. I will be dead before it can grow up again so beautiful.'

He wouldn't eat his breakfast, and he wouldn't play with his toys. He didn't even care when Lucy borrowed his best clockwork train. Daddy said that William could help to put some tiles back on the roof, but William said, 'No. I don't want to do anything. I want my tree to stand up again.'

'Well, it can't,' said Daddy. He went off to fix the roof, and William just stood and looked at the poor old tree.

After a while William said, 'May I climb on it?'

'Yes,' said Daddy. And he helped him up. William sat on the trunk and held on to a high branch. 'I'm a squirrel,' he said. Daddy lifted up Lucy to be another squirrel next to him. 'Have a nut,' said William kindly, and Lucy ate a pretend nut. Then William climbed further along the tree-trunk, and found a higher branch to sit on. It felt safe and secret, up among the leaves. 'The tree is still my friend,' he said.

There wasn't any electricity all day, because the wind had knocked down all the poles and wires. 'It must have been a hurricane,' said Mummy. At lunchtime, they had to make a fire of branches and leaves, and cook sausages on it. 'We're cooking on a wood fire,' said William. 'Just like in the old days when my tree was little.' He took his sausages and sat on the big tree-trunk to eat them. 'Will we have to have a candle to light us to bed?'

'Yes, I think so,' said Mummy. 'And a lantern, to eat our supper by.'

William and Lucy played on the tree all day long. When it was nearly dark, Mummy lit some candles and lanterns and the children came into the kitchen. William did a painting of the tree, and hung it on the wall. Then he said to his daddy,

'Can we plant another beech tree, just like the old one?'

'Yes,' said Daddy. 'But it won't be big for years and years.'

'I know,' said William. 'But I'd still like to plant one, please.'

Daddy was pleased. 'We'll find a good place and plant a young tree. But we'll have to look after it properly while it's little. It can be a present for your children when you grow up, and then in a hundred years, your great-grandchildren can play under the tree with all their friends.'

'And climb it?' said William.

'When they're big enough,' said Daddy. 'Anyway, every year the new tree will get bigger and stronger and more beautiful.'

'Will the hundred-years children know it was us who planted it there?' said William.

'Well,' said his daddy. 'They might guess it was someone who loved trees.'

William broke off a little twig and took it up to bed with him.

'Tomorrow we'll start to saw up the tree and tidy it away,' said his daddy. 'But wood is useful stuff. If we save it carefully, and dry it for a year, we'll be able to make new things out of it, in my workshop.'

'A chair for the kitchen,' said Mummy.

'And a toy boat,' said Lucy.

'And a desk for my work,' said Daddy. 'What would you like, William?'

William thought for a minute. 'I want a rocking-horse. Then I can rock on it and pretend I'm a bird on a high branch, and think about the tree that fell down in the hurricane.'

'I'll make you the best rocking-horse in the world,' said Daddy.

And he did.

This story is by Libby Purves.

Orion Hardy

Up in the hill country stands a little stone farmhouse I know very well, for I used to play hide-and-seek around the haystacks in the fenced stackyards, and I helped to drive up the cows from the long sloping fields which dip down to the valley.

It was a farm I liked very much because there was a romantic feeling about the place. It stood, sturdy and strong, with thick grey stone walls against the hill, and its smiling face peered down to the valley seven hundred feet below. At night it was like a lighthouse in the darkness, with one small light beaming from its windows.

I ran down the fields to that valley, down and down, as swiftly as the wind, till I came to the little brown brook at the bottom. I climbed the stiles and chased the squirrels in the woods, and scampered along the grassy track. Then, high above me, I could see one little attic window looking down at me from the farmhouse roof, and I waved my hand in goodbye.

The farm had had several owners who had left for one thing and another. This was strange in a countryside where people stayed at their farms for a hundred years. It had the reputation of being unlucky. It was quite true that queer things happened there, but when I knew it the luck had come back and there was content. This is how it happened.

One day an old farm labourer walked up the fields with his bundle on his back and a stick in his hand. When he came to the gate of the farmyard he stood for a while leaning there, watching the house, and the house seemed to gaze back at him.

Then out came Farmer Holland, with his barking dogs at his heels. The dogs rushed forward and then wagged their tails and leapt joyously at the old man.

'What do you want? Have you lost your way?' asked the farmer.

'Have you work for me, Master?' asked the old man, and he opened the gate and walked slowly into the yard. 'I'm looking for a place, for I'm all alone now. I've been used to farming all my life, but I've been in London for a long time. I couldn't abide the pavements any more, so I've come back to the land where I belong.'

The farmer looked keenly at the hesitating old fellow, whose hands were trembling with excitement.

'Yes, I've plenty of work, plenty, but I doubt if you'd do for me. You're an old man, and it's a hard place here,' said Farmer Holland.

The old man's face drooped and his blue eyes dimmed with disappointment. Then little Tom Holland came running from the fields, hurrying to find out why the dogs had barked and the gate clicked. He stopped suddenly when he saw the stranger, but the old man crooked a finger and nodded to him in a friendly way, and Tom came forward and stood at his side.

The barn-door cock flew to the low wall of the grass-plat and crowed a welcoming 'Cock-a-doodle-doo!' A cuckoo called 'Cuckoo! Cuckoo!' from the walnut tree in the croft. The cat sidled from the stackyard and brushed the man's corduroys with her curling tail. A robin hopped near with inquisitive eye and then sang a cascade of music.

'Can you plough and sow? Can you reap and mow? Can you thatch a barn and mend a wall? Are you a bit of a vet, and can you look after horses?' asked the farmer, with a touch of scorn.

'Yes, Master, I can do all those things,' replied the old man simply, with no boasting.

'And you've not forgot, in London?' asked the farmer.

'We never forget,' said the old man, proudly.

'Well, I'll take you on till the harvest is over, and after that I'll make no promises. I'll see how you shape yourself.'

'Thank you, Master. Thank you. You won't regret it.' The old man spoke softly.

'See if you can earn your keep. It's hard to make a living here, what with one thing and another.'

'Yes, Master. Hard living doesn't daunt me. I'm used to it.'

'What's your name?' asked the farmer as he turned back to the house, with the old man following him.

'Orion Hardy, but they calls me Rion for short,' said the old man.

'Orion. Queer name. Name of stars. Come on in, Rion.'

'Orion,' murmured little Tom, and he took the old man's hand. 'Orion, I like you.'

'Here's Rion Hardy come to help us out, wife,' shouted Farmer Holland, throwing wide the door.

'I hope you can, for we need some helping,' said a quiet little voice, and Mrs Holland smiled at the old man and her Tom.

The old man went about the day's work, and at night he retired to the attic under the roof, with his bundle of clothes, and his stick in a corner. He looked through the window, down the long fields to the valley, and he began to whistle softly.

'Here I am, with a roof over my head, and a good supper inside me, and plenty of friends in the farmyard. I shan't do so badly,' said he, aloud.

'Badly,' echoed the room.

He started and looked around.

'I shall do well,' he said, firmly.

'Well?' asked the room.

'That's better,' said he.

'Better,' said the echoing voice.

He undressed and got into bed, but in the night he was wakened by an uneasy feeling. The bedclothes were twitched from over him, and the hard little pillow was pulled from under his head. A cold wind blew on his face, and there were rustlings. All his clothes, which he had left in a neat pile, were thrown about.

'Go to sleep, there,' he cried, and he could hear elfin laughter and the strange pattering of feet.

He said nothing when Mrs Holland asked him how he slept, except 'It was a bit company-like.'

Now he noticed that the house-place was untidy, the cinders lay on the hearth, and milk was spilled on the floor. He helped to tidy it up, surprised by the mess.

'Seems as if the place is bewitched,' said Mrs Holland, sadly. 'Once I didn't believe in such things, but we have some queer goings-on. Things get lost and moved out of their places, as if somebody had a spite against us.'

'That's bad,' said Orion. 'Have you tried a branch of the wicken tree?' (The wicken tree is the rowan, which grows in hilly land.)

'Yes, I put boughs of the wicken tree over the doors, but it goes on just the same,' replied Mrs Holland.

Orion went out to the milking, and as he milked the cows he thought of the trouble at the farm and wondered what he could do. He fettled the mare and brushed up the stable, he suckled the calves and fed the pigs.

As he did the work, slowly and methodically, he forgot the farm's bad luck and the disturbances of the night in the pleasure he felt at being back with things he loved. He looked after the animals and opened the gates for them, with never a cross word when the cows blundered the wrong way, and he spoke gentle, soothing talk to the mare, and spoke to the pigs, encouraging them, as if they could understand him.

So the day went on, and little Tom Holland ran about with the new farm man, Orion, and helped him. But at night there was the same upset and disturbance, and Orion decided that he must leave the little room.

'I would like to change my bedroom if you don't mind, Missis,' he said, after he had put the attic to rights.

'We haven't another room, Rion. It's the same everywhere, worse in some than others,' said Mrs Holland.

'I'll sleep in the stable, Missis,' said Orion.

'Just as you like, Rion. Better folk than us have slept in stables, and perhaps you will find it more peaceful,' sighed the farmer's wife. 'I do wish we could get some quiet here.'

So the old man settled himself in the corner of the stable, with his bundle of clothes in the stone embrasure in the wall. He had a three-legged stool to sit on, and the mounting-block was his table. A heap of fresh golden straw, with a clean sack thrown over it, made a bed. That was all he wanted, and when the little yellow cat walked in to keep him company, and to kill the mice, he was delighted. The mare turned her head and watched him, and whinnied with joy to have him there.

Outside in the yard was the water-trough, cut out of an immense block of stone, and a spring ran into it with a singing trickle of fresh cold water. A bucket stood in the corner, and he swilled his face and dried it on his little towel. He combed his rough hair, and then he undressed by the light of a candle in the iron candlestick stuck in the wall.

Harness and bridle and bit hung from the stall, and horse brasses and martingale were fastened to the wooden beams of the roof. There was a fine horse blanket, striped red and yellow, to cover him, and his pillow was stuffed with sweet hay.

Just before he went to sleep he looked out of the door at the night sky and the stars. His own constellation, Orion, had gone, for it was early summer, but he could see the Great Bear and Cassiopeia's Chair. He could hear the water trickling into the trough, and it seemed to be saying something, but he could not catch the words. Across the yard the house was in darkness, except for the glimmer of a nightlight in little Tom's room.

'I'll make that whistle-pipe tonight, and give it him tomorrow,' said Orion. 'He's a nice little lad. He'll be right pleased to have it, and I'll play a tune to him.'

He took his clasp-knife and the piece of ash sapling he had brought with him from the fields, and by the light of the candle he cut the green bark and made the whistle-pipe.

Great shadows danced over the ceiling as he bent his head to the work, the mare turned to look at him, and the little cat rubbed against him.

'How's this, Jenny?' he asked, as he cut the last slit and made the small holes for the stops. 'Would you like a tune, lass?' He put the pipe to his lips and played an air, and the mare listened intently, flicking her ears with joy.

Horses like music, especially the sound of soft notes from wooden pipes, and Jenny gave a snuffle of admiration as the old man played his tunes. Suddenly her ears went back and her eyes showed alarm. The cat's hair stood on end. A whispering shuffling sound came from the yard, and Orion went across to the door and opened the top half.

Over the cobbles pranced a host of grey shadows. They ran on tiptoe to the house and pressed close to the walls. They threw up their arms and leapt in the air.

'Them's the disturbers,' muttered Orion. 'Wouldn't I like to upset their pranks.'

He put his whistle-pipe to his mouth again and sent a stream of music swinging through the air, strange dancing music, which set the cat leaping and the mare nodding her great head. Then out from the house came the shadows, swaying and trembling in the moonlight, over the cobbles, and away through the gate.

Orion shut the stable door and got into his bed. He put his whistle-pipe under his pillow

126

and fell fast asleep. Soon there was no sound but the soft purring of the little cat, the snores of Orion, and grunts of contentment from the mare.

The next day Orion went to the house for his breakfast. His milking was done, the mare fed, and the stable tidied. Mrs Holland was all smiles as she poured out his tea.

'No trouble last night, Orion,' she said. 'It's the first time for months. You must have brought us luck.'

'Did you make my whistle-pipe?' asked little Tom.

'Yes, Tom. Here it is. Yes, I made it last

night, when the moon was shining, and it plays well. I'll play it when I've had my bit of summat to eat.'

Little Tom was delighted, and the old man played his tunes, and made even the cat dance again.

But Orion said nothing of the night's adventures, and he made another whistle-pipe to keep ready for the shadow-folk, if they should come again. Come they did, and he turned them away, whistling to them from the stable door, beguiling them from the farmhouse.

Other strange things happened at that farm on the hill. One day the farmer's wife called to Orion.

'Go and fetch some water, Rion. You'll have to carry it from the spring yonder in the fields. The water-trough here is dry.'

Sure enough, the singing trickle of cold water had disappeared, and there was not a drop to drink.

'What has happened to it, Ma'am?' asked the old man, as he slipped the yoke over his shoulders and fastened a pair of buckets to the chains.

'It dries up each year in summer, like this, and leaves us with never a drop.'

'It ought not to do that, Ma'am,' said Orion, and off he ambled across the fields with little Tom trotting by his side. As he went, he told the little boy all about water, running under the ground, and leaping up in a spring for people to drink.

'Where's our water gone?' asked Tom.

'Maybe it's got fast down there,' said Rion. He held the buckets to the trickle in the field from the silver spring that bubbled out of the ground.

'Listen,' cried Tom. 'There's somebody calling.'

'Set me free. Set me free,' sang a high, silvery voice, and Tom and Orion nodded and whispered.

'It's something down there,' said Tom.

When the buckets were full, Orion carried them back to the farm.

'That spring seems to be stopped up in the

field,' said he. 'Shall I take a spade and clear it out?'

'Waste of time,' said Farmer Holland. 'It always was a poor spring. Don't bother over it. '

When evening came, after milking was over and there was some free time, the old man returned with a spade and dug a trench. He found that a great stone had stopped up the water. It came rushing out in a clear stream, gushing like a fountain, and a voice sang, 'I am free. I am free. I am free.'

Away ran the water, diving underground again; and when Orion got back to the farm, there was a rushing waterfall in the stone trough, to serve the house and farm.

That night, when Orion went to the stable to sleep, he could hear very distinctly the voice of the water talking and singing. It laughed as it fell on the stones to cool them, it chuckled with glee. When the band of shadows came out, as usual, they danced up to the spring instead of going to the house walls, and they all stooped and drank. Then deep into the earth they all sank, and were never seen again.

It was time to reap the corn, and every day was busy. The golden wheat was cut and bound into sheaves, and the sheaves were carried to the threshing floor of the great barn. Orion took his swingle and flail to thresh some corn to be ground into flour for the household.

As he worked there alone one day he heard a voice crying, 'Don't beat me. Don't beat me.'

He stopped and listened, but there was nobody to be seen. He swung his flail again, and again a voice cried out in piteous tones, 'Don't beat me.'

He turned over the corn, and there was a fine sheaf lying on the floor, with great golden ears, heavy as if they had been pure gold. He lifted it out and set it aside, for it was the pick of all the fields. He remembered it, wheat that had grown in a favoured spot, tall, red–gold wheat. The voice stopped, and he went on with the threshing.

The farmer came to the barn and picked up

a handful of corn from the floor and let it run through his fingers. Then he noticed the fine sheaf set aside.

'Why have you left that? It's our best wheat. Get it threshed, Rion. I wanted to see its quality.'

'Nay, Master. I put it aside for the Harvest Thanksgiving. I'll make a good neat sheaf of it and take it to the church, for it's lovely corn.'

'I don't send anything there, Rion. It's good corn, and we need it.'

'Master, let me bind it afresh and take it down, for we've had a good harvest and we ought to give thanks.'

'Have it your own way, Rion,' said Farmer Holland, turning away. 'You always get your own way; and I will say this, things haven't been so bad lately.'

So Rion bound the sheaf with a twisted band of straw and carried it down to the church for the Harvest Festival. The vicar was much surprised, but he placed the golden sheaf right by the altar, as a thank-offering from the farm.

Little Tom went to church with his mother to see it on Sunday, but old Rion kept away.

'I'm not fine enough,' said he. 'I give my thanks to God in the stable and in the fields. That's where I belong.'

The harvest was over, and the old man prepared to go on his way. He was slower than ever, and he felt that the farmer would never keep him through the winter months when there was not much work to be done. So he packed his bundle one morning and came before the farmer.

'I'd best be going along,' said he. 'I've been happy here. I'll maybe come back for next harvest, if you want me.'

'You're not going, Rion?' asked Farmer Holland. 'You don't want to leave us, do you?'

'No, I don't want to go, but I thought as how . . .'

'Then stop. Say no more. Why, Rion, I do believe you've changed the luck of the farm. I don't know how you managed it, but it is different now,' said the farmer.

'Stay with us, Orion,' said Mrs Holland.